The Struggle To Not Go Out Of Relevance

Shivani Ahuja

ISBN: 978-93-5321-828-7

DEDICATION

To my little world that starts and ends with love in this vast universe,

Everything I am and everything I am going to be, is because of you.

Thank you for making every battle, every victory and every fall seem effortless.

I love you.

ACKNOWLEDGMENTS

Thank you for the title, Abhinav.

PREFACE

Hi beautiful soul,

This is everything I have ever written. The first words I ever wrote was for my mom in a handwritten card, all I wrote was I love you. And maybe a drawing of me and her, she still has it in her safe. Later, I realized that the words I heard and read, stayed with me long enough to mold me as a person.

The situations in my life have made me grow up too soon, wear my heart on my sleeve and most importantly, love.

From the 8-year-old who didn't know what she was doing to the 22-year-old who is trying to put together poems hoping she makes an impact; the days to come will be filled with love and light.

And to you, who holds this book, I hope you find comfort and light in these words.

1. YOU TOO

I know, you too, just like me, stay up,

for all the dreams you see at night are

better than the ones you live.

You too, just like me are joining the barbed wire

around your heart, for the world won't be strong

enough to see you bleed.

You too, just like me, silently ache for the ones that

were snatched away from you, for the world won't ever

think you're enough to love.

I know it all, too well enough to know where you wish to stay.

I know that your grief is the piece of clothing that

has stitched itself on your soul.

I know that you too, just like me,

will fight, with everything you have.

And you'll always have me.

2. A LOVE LIKE MINE

I will not love like it

hangs by a thin thread.

A thread that is woven with

the things you do for me;

I don't know a love like that.

My love is like

the sun loves the sky,

light up our worlds

and never owe each other

anything.

3. FORGETFULNESS

You see,

I often forget to remember that I can forget.

It hit me that I won't be able to

hear you laugh again

I won't be able to hug

you a minute longer again

I won't be able to love

your seven smiles again.

You see,

I often forget to remember that I can forget.

Tell me, do you still

prefer tea over coffee?

Tell me, do your eyes

still sparkle when you smile?

Tell me, is there an eighth smile

I can fall for all over again?

You, see,

I often forget to remember that I can forget.

4. RELIGION

If you really want to follow a religion,

let it be love.

Love makes you a consciously rethink
your actions.

Love makes you a better person

and makes you look forward to tomorrows.

Love makes our worlds beautiful.

It isn't warring between colors or faith
or forcing you to make it your own.

 Love just makes you better.

If you really want to follow a religion,

let it be love.

5. CLOTHING

You wear love

like I wear grief.

Turning the world blind

and yet

hiding behind it.

6. A LIFTIME OR THREE

What if,

I told a stranger that it'll take me

a lifetime or three to believe again?

These strangers want to know what I do to earn my bread and butter;

they want to know which my favorite movie is;

they want to know where I go when I feel blue.

I don't think they matter.

I wish I could show them that here's what has shattered my faith,

here's why I keep joining barbed wires around my heart

and it will take a lot for them to shackle.

If you, out of all the people couldn't learn my language of love;

I don't think anyone else will.

What if,

I told a stranger that it'll take me

a lifetime or three to believe again?

7. HOW DO YOU SPELL LOVE?

What language is it?

Is it loud?

Is it only soothing to my eyes?

Is it soft on the surface?

Is it harsh with all the coziness on the inside?

Is it in everything you do?

Is it braille?

Do I need to caress your heart to learn it?

Do your eyes talk?

Should I never stop stealing glances from you?

Is it silent?

I'll hold you only to hold you forever.

Is it in every breath you take?

I'll be with you till the last one.

Tell me,

how do you spell love?

8. OF HOPES AND DREAMS

I've got no hopes

tied to what

we're holding on to.

For tomorrow,

you'll be a dream

I'll never be able to

dream again.

9. NOT SAVED

"What's not saved will be lost."

Point in focus, everything.

Whether it is yourself, your relations, your work and your money.

Everything is spent, including you.

Firstly,

no one is taking their money to their grave.

Secondly,

by not saving what you care about, you're a loser.

Thirdly,

if you are not happy, no one can make you happy.

Spend yourself in the name of love,

it's worth the investment.

10. HOME

The kind of home

I'll build someday,

won't just have four walls

and

a roof.

Each brick will

have warmth.

Each wall will

echo with laughter.

Each corner will be

a safe one.

Each door will welcome

you with open arms.

Each room will help you

find a purpose.

11. WITNESS

Look at you,

Painting a brave face to mask the way your skin shrinks when you call it your own again.

I am sorry for the courage you must show.

I am sorry for the way you were forced to learn the manners of healing before you had time to hurt.

I promise you emptiness; you fill it with all the screams you swallowed, all the bleeding you staunched because you were too afraid to leave inedible stains.

I promise you faith; you make me whatever you wish for me to be.

I promise you love: that will always envelope you when darkness surrounds you.

Let it hurt; let it pour out of you in waves of anger and grief you were never allowed to.

Let your pain untangle around you.

I'll stand as your witness.

12. THE JOBS

There are jobs assigned to each one of us,

You know?

There's a mother,

who can't cry.

There's a father,

who can't dream.

There's a son,

who can't love.

There's a daughter,

who can't live.

Where can we resign?

13. IT'S NOT YOUR JOB

No, love.

It's not your job

to make me

feel okay.

It's not your job

to hold me,

That's my job.

It's my job

to keep standing there

with all my love,

waiting for you to

maybe,

love you with all I have

if you needed it.

14. DUST OF HELPLESSNESS

Every night,

I talk to the moon about you.

We talk about

how you used

to smile.

I can't forgive

myself for

forgetting

what your laugh

sounded like.

Every morning,

a dream of you

wakes me up.

I look for you

and eventually

go back to sleep,

only to find you.

Every morning,

I make coffee

just the way

you liked it.

Maybe,

this is my way

of keeping you

with me;

with a dust of helplessness.

15. A DIFFERENT LIFE

Every now and then,

it's a different life.

You're in your crisp white shirt,

walking towards me and

telling me that this is real.

Every now and then,

it's a different life.

A life where you and I

start the day together.

Every now and then,

it's a different life.

Where I want to sit you

 down and see your eyes

sparkle as you smile.

Every now and then,

it's a different life.

I fight for you.

16. WONDER

You know,

I wonder

how you'd laugh

when I dance.

I wonder,

if you'd get up

at 4 am just

because I did.

I wonder,

if you'd smile

silly when I

make bad coffee.

I wonder,

if you'd

sing with me

while I am drunk.

I wonder,

if you'd still

look at me

like I am your

beautiful little girl.

17. SUPERHERO

My superhero

doesn't wear a cape.

My superhero

loves.

My superhero

saves unknowingly.

My superhero

holds my hand

as I stand tall on

my two feet.

My superhero

doesn't even know

that he is one.

18. FAMILIAR

When it comes to you,
the world is not even an option.

Ironically,

I fall short of words,

when it comes to you.

When it comes to you,

the darkness fades away.

I don't know how,

but when you walk by,

the whole world stops,

my heart skips a beat

and it's only you that my

eyes are familiar with.

It's only you.

19. REDEFINING TOGETHER

It is beautiful to know

that we will

always be here

to see each other

grow.

Miles away,

my heart has

a new address.

We'll always

witness every fall,

every rise

and still keep

each other sane.

I'd choose distance,

if it was with you.

20. IT'S US AGAINST THE WORLD

Every now and then,

worlds collapse, that's the law.

Somehow, there have been loves that

haven't left without leaving.

Either taken a piece of me or left a piece of them,

they stay because I let them.

There is a world I built,

a world where we cuddle up and watch movies every evening,

a world that starts with pancakes and coffee,

a world where love is a language we're fluent in,

and it's enough.

It's us against the world.

21. YOUR DOORSTEP

Destiny placed me at

your doorstep.

I knocked,

unsure of what's

on the other side.

Destiny placed me at

your doorstep.

I found a familiar heart,

and the purest smile.

Destiny placed me at

your doorstep.

All I could do

was love you,

and it never seemed

enough.

22. THE STRUGGLE TO NOT GO OUT OF RELEVANCE

Hey, you, pause for a minute.

Breathe.

As much as your job fills your bank accounts and your stomach,

does it fill your heart?

As much as your ego feeds your pride,

does it make you smile?

As much as the world takes away from you,

does it give you something in return?

As much as the love you give away,

does it come back your way?

That my friend,

is the struggle to not go out of relevance.

Breathe.

THANK YOU

33

I've been told I have a way with words
and I am really hoping that I do.

Thank you, for your time and all the love.

This is me, hoping that these words
made you smile but mostly, feel.

Hope you're always surrounded by love and light every day.

"Trust me, putting your job ahead
 of your heart is a mistake.
Risking our hearts is why we're alive."

ABOUT THE AUTHOR

In the 2 decades and 2 years I have spent on this planet, I have spent most of my time loving the mere idea of love.

Social media pays my bills and poetry fills my heart.

I have been told that I have a way with words and this is me, hoping you find a little part of you in my words.

This is everything I've dreamt of and of course, the struggle is to not go out of relevance.

35